HOW TO BECOME THE GO-TO PERSON

MAKE YOURSELF INDISPENSABLE!

Norah Deay

Copyright © 2015 by Norah Deay

All rights reserved. No part of this publication may be reproduced, distributed, or transmitted in any form or by any means, including photocopying, recording, or other electronic or mechanical methods, without the prior written permission of the publisher, except in the case of brief quotations embodied in critical reviews and certain other non-commercial uses permitted by copyright law.

This book is dedicated to my husband, Michael, who has always believed I could do anything I wanted once I set my mind to it, even when I didn't quite believe it.

Table of Contents

Introduction

FIRST IMPRESSIONS

THE CURSE THAT IS THE TOXIC PERSON

BE A POSITIVE FORCE

THE EARLY BIRD

ASK QUESTIONS

BE QUICK TO RESPOND

DRESS TO IMPRESS

ASK FOR HELP

NO SURPRISES

OWN YOUR MISTAKES

GET INVOLVED

BE PASSIONATE ABOUT WHAT YOU DO

TAKE OWNERSHIP

MAKE THINGS HAPPEN

BE INTERESTED

SAY YES

EMOTIONAL INTELLIGENCE

HARD WORK

SPECIALISING

FURTHER LEARNING

STRESS

BEST FOOT FORWARD

RESOURCES

Introduction

DISCLAIMER: The hero of this book is a female. Primarily, because the majority of the Go-To people are administrative staff and the majority of these people are women.

Though, I'm very aware that there are loads of male admin staff, but for easier reading, I'm going with one gender throughout this eBook.

One of my favourite TV programs is Suits, the legal drama. Not for the legal shenanigans that occupy the main characters every week but rather for Donna, the fabulously organised fount of all knowledge who stalks the halls of power on impossible heels.

Donna can fix everything, from making sure her lawyer is where he's supposed to be, to mending his broken heart. If you're the type of person who admires this style, then this book is for you.

If you value being necessary at work, this book is for you. If you're just starting out and are intimidated by the Donnas of the corporate world, this book is for you. And if you want to give yourself a refresher course on how you got to be so Donna-like, then this book is definitely for you.

Why would you want to be the person that everyone comes to for help? Surely this would mean long hours and stress that you don't either want or need? No, it doesn't have to be that way. You will have developed a reputation for helping people and because you're doing them a favour in most cases, they're willing to wait for you.

I bluffed my way into my first secretarial job in London in the late 80s. I'd owned a community newsletter back in Ireland so my typing skills were pretty good, but I didn't have a clue about working in an office. My sister's husband owned a company and they provided a reference for me. I wouldn't advocate doing that now – it's too easy to be caught out!

I was 27 years old when I arrived in London and most of my contemporaries were already well established in their careers but I took a junior role to get my foot on the ladder (I was earning $7,000 a year! That's almost unimaginable today.) and within a short space of time I had another job with a lot more money.

Nearly thirty years later, I've had wonderful jobs (and of course, some not so wonderful) spread over four countries on two continents.

Being a personal assistant has given me a good working life and always being the go-to person has made my working life special.

Being a PA or EA is a great career if you want it to be. It's entirely mobile so you can work in a lot of different industries, in a lot of different places. Although I talk about administrators in the book, I assume that most administrators want to work their way up the career ladder to become a Personal or Executive Assistant and that's who this book is aimed at.

People who want to know what they need to know to make themselves indispensable and get those promotions and salary increases. It's not enough these days to just turn up at work. You're expected to be a contributor also.

I've had some wonderful jobs. I've worked for a fabulous cosmetics company (one word - samples), a prestigious real estate company, a powerful semi-state body and best employer of all, myself.

It's not that I really like work, but I'm very good at it. At twenty-three I had a failed marriage and a baby son and I was living with my parents. I had no qualifications, so it made complete sense to take out a bank loan to pay for a private six-week secretarial course. Seven weeks later, I landed my first secretarial job.

My nature is such that I always want to be the best at what I do so I set out to make myself the very best personal assistant I could be and this story and experience is what I want to share with you. How to go from being a junior who doesn't know what they don't know, to being a person who has all the answers to the questions others don't know.

I wasn't polished or elegant. I was well read but not well educated. I had very little confidence in myself, but not many people knew that. If you're shy or have little confidence change your passwords to an affirmation e.g. <u>I am a confident person</u>. I guarantee that by the time you've typed that a hundred times you **will** feel more confident.

I left school at sixteen and worked in a series of minimum wage jobs in small town Ireland until my mid-twenties. By the time I was 30 years old, I was living in London and was a Personal Assistant to the Managing Director of a company who designed lighting for some of the most exciting new buildings in the city.

I can promise that if you follow the advice in this book, you will find yourself in the position of being the go-to person in your organisation. Who you want to be afterwards is up to you because one of the great things about being the Go-To person is that you can set your sights on your boss' job if that's what you want.

One of the things I talk about in the book is how to avoid procrastination, so I will start here by saying there's never a better time to begin than today.

How many times do you see books like this advertised and think it's not for me? <u>I'm too old </u>or<u> I'm too tired to get enthused again</u>. Nonsense! I believe anyone can change if they have the will, and want to.

I will show you how the principles that apply to a junior can also apply to someone with twenty years' experience.

No matter where you are on your life journey, it's never too late to start over. In reality, every time we get out of bed in the morning we're starting over.

Becoming a Go-to person is not going to be easy if you're only known for being grumpy and unhelpful. This is where

I advise changing jobs. Sometimes you really do have to start over – it can be very difficult to reinvent yourself if you have to build bridges with everyone first.

I'd love to say that I have always practiced what I preach here but some of it has come from mistakes made and lessons learned, so don't be daunted if you feel you could do better. That's why you're reading this book.

Let's get started.

FIRST IMPRESSIONS

"Smiling can be a competitive advantage. It makes everyone feel better and every situation brighter.

"Richard Branson"

One of the most commonly used expressions regarding first impressions is that you don't get a second chance to make them. Don't waste the first impressions you make on your first day in the new job.

You don't get a do-over, there won't be a second chance.

It's the first morning in your new job and you're sitting nervously in the reception area waiting for someone to show you where to go. A sea of faces passes by. Most, if not all, will ignore you but occasionally someone will glance your way and you'd better be ready with <u>that</u> smile.

The smile that says "I come in peace" or "I am a nice person and mean you no harm".

We all make judgement calls on people when we first see them and our reaction depends on how that person responds to us. It doesn't matter if you're one of the nicest people on the planet, if nobody knows about it because you never smile.

The first person and often the most influential to new starters is the receptionist. Make friends with her. Other people will ask her about you, who you are, what she thinks of you. They will use this information to make their decisions about you.

You don't want a bad reputation before you've even started, just because she thinks you're "not very friendly".

Waft to your new desk on a sea of goodwill. Imagine your first day is like a savings account - you need to make deposits to receive interest.

From the moment you arrive, you will be judged - don't ever think that you won't. Sometimes, it is sub-conscious but it'll always be there. Your peers will check you out to see if you're a threat. Can you make them look bad? You may be more accomplished than them in one or many skills, but the trick is to share your knowledge in a way that is helpful and not condescending.

Don't forget that you're the new girl and you have to earn your place in the hierarchy.

Your boss and their peers will judge you to see how useful you're going to be to them. They judge you on your demeanour - are you friendly? helpful? calm? - and on your competence.

There's no point in competence and experience without warmth and of course there's no point in being everyone's best friend if you're useless at your job.

Nothing peeves women so much as having the new girl ignore them in favour of the men in the office. You're dealing with emotions and how you make people feel. Make friends with the women first and then you can make friends with the men.

Is this politically incorrect? Of course it is, but incorrect or not it's still a fact that people (not only women) are upset when they feel dismissed and not only will you not become the Go-To person, you will become the Don't-Go-To person.

It's not a difficult thing to be nice, but sometimes people get so nervous about the job itself they can forget their natural skills. The work will still be there tomorrow, but tomorrow will be too late to make a first impression.

That's Day 1 over and you go home feeling you've done what you needed to in order to make a good impression and maybe you feel like you've made a friend or two.

But what happens if your new best friend turns out to be a toxic person?

THE CURSE THAT IS THE TOXIC PERSON

"Save your skin from the corrosive acids from the mouths of toxic people. Someone who just helped you to speak evil about another person can later help another person to speak evil about you."

Israelmore Ayivor

Toxic people have usually been with the company for a reasonable length of time and haven't progressed very far. This is not their fault. They are misunderstood, overworked and underpaid according to them and if you allow them space in your head you will become disillusioned as well.

You'll notice things that annoy you, irritate you and generally make you wonder if this is really your dream job after all.

Toxic people are lethal because they usually seem really fun to have around. There's lots of laughter and jokes until one day you realise that the jokes are always at someone else's expense. It's a good idea to keep your eyes and ears open for people like this so that you won't be sucked into their vortex.

You won't make enemies if you refuse to engage with this person, but you may end up being regarded as having the same faults if you do.

Keep a distance between you. Don't feel bad about this. She's a stranger and not necessary in your life. She will have her supporters so be diplomatic. You don't want to end up on their radar either.

You'll often find that this person applied for your job and is perhaps, making a point to your boss by being friendly with you. She will use any information she can extract from you to seal your fate because she really believes that she'll be a shoo-in for the job when you leave.

If you need to unload to someone make sure it's a positive person because they will help solve your problem, not multiply it.

In my first secretarial job I was advised that my boss was on her way out and if I could only put up with her for a while longer I was in the running for her job. However, my 'friend' told me over and over that she would never leave and things would never get better for me. I handed in my resignation and left. Little did I know that she was afraid her boyfriend fancied me! It really **can** be that simple.

Therefore, be careful. It takes time to get to know people and what their intentions are towards you. Don't allow your need to fit in at work, blind you to toxic people. Being aware of people like this is often more than half the battle.

Pay attention to the words and tone that people use. If they don't leave you feeling positive, you know what you have to do.

BE A POSITIVE FORCE

"The greatest discovery of any generation is that a human being can alter his life by altering his attitude."

William James

Surround yourself with positive people both inside and outside of work. Their positivity will ensure your positive outlook remains strong and you will be a person that others gravitate towards. It's not difficult, as you'll see in this chapter.

Positive people are polar opposites to Toxic People. No matter how bad the situation, they always look for the upside. This is what you're aiming for. Not only in your professional life but in your personal life as well.

Be a person that others want to be around. Be someone who can get others to listen. This happens naturally when you're a positive force.

Others gravitate towards you. They trust you and they include you. You become an integral part of the team.

Toxic People are reactive, self-centred, and fatalistic. Therefore, you need to be the opposite of all of these. You are the one who will choose to either drag people down or be the kind of person who lift others up.

In one of her books author Marian Keyes describes people as either drains or radiators. Radiators by their nature radiate warmth and comfort, while drains just keep on sucking the life out of you.

If you don't know, or are not sure, if you're a positive or negative person there is just such a quiz on Mindtools.com. See the <u>Resources section at the end of this book</u>.

Your positivity will help defend you against the toxic people. As their negativity can be contagious, so can your positivity.

The single most positive thing you can do for yourself, and others, is to smile. There's truth in the saying "Smile and the world smiles with you". A smile makes you happy, it makes others happy and it helps with stress. And best of all, it often turns to laughter.

Look for solutions. When you're asked a question you don't know the answer to, respond with "I don't know right now but I'll find out and get back to you". Never finish with "I don't know".

ALWAYS be polite. Say please and thank you.

Be kind to everyone. Not just the popular people.

Be respectful of other cultures and appreciate the opportunity to learn about the world you are part of, not just your little corner of it.

When you're positive you can gain support for your ideas. You gain a reputation as someone to be trusted. You become a role model for others to emulate and this translates into promotions and higher salaries.

As you read you may feel that negativity has taken over your life. You hate your job, you're not very fond of your colleagues, you feel nothing is ever going to change for you.

You can choose to change this. I believe we start over every morning we're lucky enough to wake up. If you hate your job so much you can't envisage it getting any better, change it. The power is in your own hands.

Even if the unemployment situation is bad where you are you can begin preparing for that great job you're going to have. It may take a lot of effort and determination to implement these changes in your life. Believing you can change is the first step to a more positive you.

Practise smiling if you've forgotten how to do it. Think about the reference you'd like to receive and start working towards it. Up your game. Take an online course – see the <u>Resources section at the end of this book</u>.

You never know - you might discover a newfound enjoyment in your work and not need to chase another job.

THE EARLY BIRD

"You've got to get up every morning with determination if you're going to go to bed with satisfaction."

George Lorimer

Being early is what successful people do. Unless you're a rock star you will never get rich lying in bed until Midday. Being early is my thing. I don't believe I'd have been as successful if I hadn't been an early riser.

From Day Two onwards, you need to be in the office at least half an hour before anyone else. More if possible.

If you're used to going out socializing until the early hours' mid-week you might want to have a rethink if you're serious about a career.

Eau de stale booze is not attractive, add in bleary eyes and make-up residue and you will not get any interesting or difficult work to do - because you won't be trusted to do it properly. Would you trust yourself?

Getting into the habit of rising early is one of the most productive, energising things you'll ever do for yourself.

Crisp winter or balmy summer mornings look even better when there are fewer people around. You feel inspired and alive and even though you may have had less sleep than you'd like, you can feel much more awake.

Be early. Be earlier than everyone else. Be so consistently early that if you come in on time, people will think you're late.

You can get a head start on the work you didn't do yesterday or a project that needs you to concentrate. With no interruptions, it will be much easier.

This is the time when you can check your personal emails or Facebook. Let's not pretend this doesn't happen and at least this way you're still on your own time.

Whatever you use the time for it's not being taken out of your working day so you've got a great start before anyone else is even in the office.

It will be noticed over time and you'll find people coming to you from other departments for assistance because you're the only one there.

Your nice self will always be happy to help and, like flower seeds blowing in the wind, word will spread that you're a helpful person. In other words, a Go-To person.

On a practical level, if you always have some hours in the bank and need to leave the office early it shouldn't be a problem. (I'm assuming you work for a reasonable employer).

I've always believed that I'm late if I'm not early. Being 'on time' puts you on the back foot before you even start your day. And if you're one of those people who is always 15 minutes late...

LEAVE HOME 15 MINUTES EARLIER

Learning the importance of being early is key to a successful career in administration. Getting in early helps your day get off to a great start.

ASK QUESTIONS

"I never learn anything talking. I only learn when I ask questions."

Lou Holtz

Do you feel nervous about putting your hand up to ask a question in front of colleagues? You shouldn't. Nine times out of ten you're asking a question that another nervous person couldn't ask.

There definitely is such a thing as a stupid question, but not when it comes to your new job. The biggest breakthrough is always when you begin to realise what you don't know. That's when you ask questions that mean something to you.

If you can, spend a few days studying your predecessor's work. Make notes about what you don't understand or need clarification on. Answers to these questions will now make more sense to you than if you'd been given the self-same information on your first day.

Don't be afraid to ask when you don't know something. If you don't ask and end up making a mistake that's when you will look stupid, and arrogant to think that you could do the task without assistance. I bet a lot of people would be surprised to learn that they suffer from arrogance.

They don't want to admit they don't know everything and that's a mistake that will dog them throughout their working lives. We all know such people and they always end up with egg on their face at some point in their career.

Ask for help, and listen to the answers.

Ask for clarification, and listen to the answers.

Don't spend time thinking about what you're going to say next. Just listen.

If you think you might not remember, write it down. This job is about accumulating knowledge.

The more answers you have, the more questions you will be asked.

Because that's the other side of this coin. Everything you learn is available to share with your peers. Give it freely.

Holding onto information will not raise your value to the organisation.

Asking questions can be daunting but if you approach the actual task of asking as another skill you're learning, it won't seem so difficult.

BE QUICK TO RESPOND

"It is literally true that you can succeed best and quickest by helping others to succeed."

Napoleon Hill

We're working on building your reputation as an indispensable Go-To person and one of the things, maybe the main thing, Go-To people are known for, is their timely responsiveness to requests.

The consequences of not responding quickly or as is often the case, not at all, is that you won't be asked again. That's great if you just want to show up at work but it's not at all what a Go-To person wants.

Be quick to respond. Learn to prioritise but a general rule of thumb is that anything with a deadline must be done first. I couldn't tell you the number of times I've watched people insist on finishing the *Business as Usual* task while owners of urgent tasks bite their nails to the quick in frustration.

If something is going to take 5 minutes to do, break away from the project you're working on and do it. Apart from the kudos you get for a job well done quickly, you have the satisfaction of a job completed.

What happens if you're working on something really urgent for someone outside your team and an email from your manager pops up requiring you to do something that's not time-sensitive for them?

There are lots of conflicting opinions about this, loads of articles written on "how to say NO politely" etc. The fact of the matter is; it all depends on your manager.

If they are a person who expects instant attention, then you drop what you're doing and focus on them. *Even if it seems unreasonable. You have to work with them day in, day out; don't sabotage your relationship to look like the good guy for someone from another department.*

If they are easy going and approachable explain what you're doing and tell them, you'll do their work as soon as you're finished.

Either way, the outcome must be that you feel you made the right decision.

If you're dealing with external customers, there is **no** task that's more important than theirs. They are the people who give your company its reputation so if they're unlucky enough to make a request of someone who can't multitask and prioritise then you're going to see bad reviews on the company's Facebook page.

If you regularly receive the same queries, write up a standard response that you can quickly paste into an email (like a custom reply). That will take less than a minute of your time but the customer will react as if it were a manuscript.

If the request is difficult or time consuming, do not put it off. I've always tried to do the hard jobs first - that way they're done and dusted and I don't have to think about them again.

Don't become paralysed by inaction if you've got heaps of competing tasks. Talk to the owners and work out what is **really** a priority, and work accordingly. Communication is critical to your success.

On the other hand, often you are the one who needs to ask others for assistance in order to complete a task of your own. A Harvard study in 2013 discovered the power of using the word 'Because' to get things done.

So, if you need a spreadsheet from the Finance team in order to finish a presentation for your boss make sure you ask politely and explain what you want *because* your manager needs it urgently. When someone helps you like this, they're usually doing it for you and not for your manager. Make sure you appreciate that.

Never spend time wondering who else should be doing this task - while you're wondering, you could have done it yourself.

You're learned now that not all tasks are urgent, and how to deal with those that are. Don't put work off if it's difficult and communicate, communicate, communicate.

DRESS TO IMPRESS

"You cannot climb the ladder of success dressed in the costume of failure."

Zig Ziglar

Whether you are a secretary, administrator or personal assistant you're expected to look good. You don't have to dress in haute couture with full make-up, but you do have to dress smartly. Actually you can't ever be too well-dressed in these roles. This shouldn't be a problem, most of us love clothes.

Stay away from lace and velvet for day-wear (unless you have an Austin Powers thing going on and it was evident at your interview), and stick to the dress code of the company.

You should always ask what the dress code is at your interview and if they have a Casual Friday policy.

Unless you're going to work at Google, Casual Friday usually means Smart-Casual. **Not** ripped jeans or board shorts and you may be proud of your boobs but don't turn up in a halter top. If in doubt, study what the others in your office are wearing.

A good foundation, mascara, blusher and lipstick is all most of us need. If you're over 40 do not wear black (or dark) eyeliner on your lower lid - it ages you. If you're wearing heavy eyeshadow, go for a nude lipstick. If your lipstick is shocking pink or ruby red, stick with a subtle eye colour.

If your skirt is so short you worry when you sit down, don't wear it to work again.

It doesn't matter if you're not into designers or are not a fashion plate - I'm not and never have been. My taste is more bohemian than chic but that can still look smart.

Simply put, dressing well gives you confidence and when you're confident you do a better job.

If you want to be taken seriously, dress professionally. If you're not sure what that is, Google is your friend. If you don't have much money visit the charity shops, particularly the ones in wealthy areas. You'll be surprised at what you find. Some of my best buys have come from Op shops in the nicer parts of the city.

ASK FOR HELP

"I think there are those individuals who are intimidated by really smart, talented people. But for me, surrounding yourself with great talent is the key to success."

Monika Chiang

Don't be intimidated by your peers. Emulate the more senior assistants, ask them for help and if possible ask one of them to become your mentor.

It's my experience that although that Donna creature may seem aloof, she is almost always nice with it. She has nothing to prove and because she's still a helpful person, time permitting, she will help you too.

This is a situation where the toxic people come out in force, so be aware. Be very, very aware. Trust your own instincts and ignore them. They will try to put you off associating with the senior people because of jealousy.

Emulating someone you admire is not losing track of who you are. Rather, it's discovering for yourself what qualities are present in a person who is successful doing what you do. Study how they work and interact with people at all levels.

There's an old saying about a mentor's hindsight becoming your foresight - learn from the mistakes they share with you. *When you sit on the shoulders of giants, you will see farther than your peers.*

A mentor is by nature a positive person and if they agree to work with you, you will have someone on your side who is empathetic, kind, wise, knowledgeable and above all, respected. Your organisation will appreciate that you hitch your wagon to a shooting star.

A mentor is constantly growing. She can point you towards development opportunities and be your champion in obtaining funding and/or time to carry out your studies.

Mentors value relationships and they will work alongside you to ensure you both have a positive experience. Being a mentor is a skill and a responsibility and those who undertake the task of helping you reach your potential should always be appreciated.

Surround yourself not only with positive people but also with successful people. The people you surround yourself with generate the ideas and opinions that enter your head. Make sure these are of good quality that will enrich your life.

NO SURPRISES

The cloud never comes from the quarter of the horizon from which we watch for it.

Elizabeth Gaskell

We're programmed from an early age not to be a snitch and unfortunately, this can carry over into our working lives. You are not snitching if you make your boss aware of a problem that will affect either him or the company, or both.

Never ever put anyone else's interests before those of your manager (unless they're a fraudster and ripping off the company. I worked in a bar and an artist asked if she could paint a portrait of the staff. As it happened she painted the manager with his hand in the till – little did she know!).

Obviously if you don't know about it, you can't pre-warn them but a good Assistant keeps their ear to the ground and knows most things that go on at the office.

A boss I had in London was very surprised when I told him all of his employees were in a Lotto syndicate. It was conceivable that he would turn up one Monday morning to an empty office. Unfortunately, we never got to test that theory but he did take out Lotto insurance against the possibility.

You have to always be on the lookout for anything that will negatively impact either your manager alone, or the company. Never to the extent that you become a witch-hunter, just use your common sense to ensure there are no surprises.

Even good surprises can be problematic because a clued-in manager should know everything that's going on and they will lose face, and even feel humiliated, if it's obvious that they don't. It's a big responsibility, and it's yours.

Always, protect your manager. Always.

OWN YOUR MISTAKES

"If you make a mistake, admit it and say you're sorry. No one has ever choked to death from swallowing their pride."

Anonymous

The definition of a mistake according to Dictionary.com =
an error in action, calculation, opinion, or judgment caused by poor
reasoning, carelessness, insufficient knowledge, etc.

Just knowing they are to blame is why people don't own up to mistakes - it's painful having to admit that you're not perfect or even as good at your job as you thought you were. However, it's very unlikely that you'll make that mistake again so use it as a learning experience and it won't be all bad.

I'm evangelical about admitting mistakes. I've learned more by making them than I ever could if I'd led a mistake-free life.

We are all blessed (or cursed) with an ego defence system. It's there to protect us from the negative impacts in our lives but it shouldn't be used to protect us from our mistakes. If you hide behind this defence system, then you will have a distorted view of yourself and will lack credibility.

The most important thing about making mistakes is **owning** them. Own them and own up to them. Often, the problem is solved immediately but ignoring or denying them is a recipe for disaster. That relatively small problem can become huge or at the very least, a considerable inconvenience for your boss and a black mark against you.

Working in real estate, it was crucial to get details correct. I once made a mistake with the time of an open home and didn't find out until I opened the Sunday paper and saw that my agent was expected to be in two places at the same time. She was good but not that good!

After my heart had stopped doing somersaults I called her and within a few minutes we had someone else organised to attend in her place. If I had ignored that mistake, people would have turned up to an open home that wasn't on. It would have been a bad look all round for my agent, the company and ultimately, me.

When you own up to a mistake, always ask "What can I do to fix this?". People tend to forget this bit. We're told all the time to admit our mistakes and own up to them but you can't just walk away once you do that. You've got to fix it - how will you be the go-to person if you leave that part to someone else?

You gain respect by owning mistakes - you should obviously not expect this reaction if your mistakes outweigh your good work - but in general you gain respect, you learn, and you show that your priority is to the company and not your own ego.

The best bit of advice I was ever given was from a colleague when I'd made a typo in a legal document that changed its whole argument. She said "if you don't think you'll remember this in 20 years' time, forget about it now." Of course, I do remember it but only for the advice.

Therefore, once you've owned up and hopefully rectified the situation, put it behind you and move on. There's an element of fair play in acknowledging the mistake; if it's a public mistake your boss will have to bear the brunt of the customer's anger/frustration/whatever so the least you can do is share the load.

Above all, being honest shows you have integrity, accountability and a sense of responsibility.

Accountability is about being responsible for what you do or don't do. By all means, take the credit if it's a good thing but don't go looking for someone to shove blame onto if you get it wrong. It's an unattractive trait and won't win you any friends.

Plus, your boss will mistrust you, and there goes your relationship. Although it might seem like it at the time, making a mistake is not the end of your good relationship with your boss. Avoiding the accountability for that mistake is what will destroy the relationship - that's a mistake you don't ever want to make.

GET INVOLVED

"Individual commitment to a group effort - that is what makes a team work, a company work, a society work, a civilization work."

Vince Lombardi

Getting involved is a sure-fire way to get known as the Go-To person. Get involved in everything, from helping out at reception if they're short staffed to becoming the Events Committee of one.

There's a chance that you've become so good at your job people begin to take you for granted and as any woman will tell you, we don't like being taken for granted! So what do you do about it? How do you raise your profile so that you become visible again?

This is important because if you become invisible you will get passed over for projects and awards and even promotion.

The answer is to stick your fingers into every pie you can. In other words, get involved. Attend buzz meetings, business information sessions, Friday night drinks, morning teas. It might sound as if you won't have time to do your job, but these are all important ways to become a known entity in your organisation.

The first thing to do is to build a network. You will have started doing this already just by being helpful but make a point of talking to these people in the lift or the lunch room.

Find out what they're working on and if you share an interest that's not part of your current job description, offer your services. It needs to be said, **don't take on what you can't deliver** but you can help out where you can.

The Christmas party is always a good project for getting to know people. Offer to help the committee, if there is one, or become the committee yourself if necessary. Organise team events for your department - it can be as simple as a sweep-stake for the Kentucky Derby, the Melbourne Cup or the Grand National.

Remember, people judge you on how you make them feel. If you extend your help to ensuring they enjoy their workday, you will be visible and appreciated.

Companies are becoming more involved in giving back to the community and this is a great way for you to organize your team's contribution such as street-collecting for charity or helping out at a refuge for the homeless.

Apart from raising your profile, there's an immense feel-good factor to really getting involved instead of just throwing money in a collection can.

There will be times when your job will be less busy - these are the times to offer your services to other departments and colleagues. Don't let yourself become bored - autonomy depends on your being able to fill your time at work productively.

BE PASSIONATE ABOUT WHAT YOU DO

"Your work is going to fill a large part of your life, and the only way to be truly satisfied is to do what you believe is great work. And the only way to do great work is to love what you do."

Steve Jobs

It's a long, long day if you don't like what you do. If you hate your job you are in danger of becoming a toxic person, so watch for this. If you're only in need of a holiday, take one. You're doing no good for either yourself or your boss if you're tired, cranky or just plain over it.

Be passionate about what you do.

Do you read that sentence and roll your eyes? How could anyone be passionate about this job? It's not as if you're a surgeon saving lives every day. The world's not going to come to an end just because you forgot to order Post-It notes.

Well no, the world won't come to an end but it may cause inconvenience and while it's a tiny thing in the great scheme of things, it puts a negative beside your name. Your team may not even realise they're doing it but deep down they'll have made a mental note that they must check to see if things have been done.

That's not how you get to be the Go-To person.

You have to prove that you're trustworthy and on top of things. In an office, that can be simple as ordering Post-It notes.

People who are passionate about their job today will more than likely have had the same attitude towards everything they've ever done. I've been a nanny, a supermarket checkout operator, a dispatch worker in a meat factory, barmaid, door-to-door sales of encyclopaedias, basically you name it, I've done it.

The common denominator in all those roles was that I did everything better than I thought I could. This was more for me than it was for the company. I got no sense of satisfaction at the end of the day otherwise.

If you don't have passion, you'll be bored and everyone will know it. If you are unsure about the word passion, you can call it motivation - are you motivated to do a good job? Do you bring the same positive attitude to everything you do?

If you're passionate about your work you feel energized, which in turn leads to better performance which leads to more confidence and all of this contributes towards a general sense of well-being.

The more passionate/motivated you are about your work the more payback you will receive, in salary, promotions and best of all, personal satisfaction. Be the very best you can be.

TAKE OWNERSHIP

"Happiness does not come from doing easy work but from the afterglow of satisfaction that comes after the achievement of a difficult task that demanded our best."

Theodore Isaac Rubin

A task for which you're being held accountable is usually a difficult one. Embrace these when they come along because these are your learning curves. These are tasks that will cause people to point to you and say "well done". Make a decision before you start about the outcome you want to achieve. Your attitude at the beginning will determine the outcome at the end.

One of the biggest annoyances I've encountered over the years is people getting fed up with a task and leaving it to someone else to complete. If you're given a task that is monotonous or complicated or the outcome depends on contributions from a number of other people, you have to stick with it. You have to get it done.

Remember the "<u>because</u>" provision in your question when you're asking for information. Be like a dog with a bone. Don't let it go until there is an outcome. Sometimes the outcome is not what you (or your boss) expected but that's not a reason to falter. Nothing matters so long as you complete the task.

The implications of not finishing are that you will have it hanging over you, causing you irritation and stress. You will shy away from questions about your progress, causing distrust and disappointment in your work. If you can't do this job just because it's difficult you won't be asked again and will miss out on opportunities, which you might have enjoyed.

If you see something wrong that would take five minutes to fix don't tell someone else to do it if you already know how - e.g. a database needs updating and you know what is required, but you pass it on to someone who is 'responsible' for it. While you're writing that email with instructions you could have done it yourself.

Owning a task is about accountability. From the beginning to the end you will be responsible for the outcome. You will know why it is important and the ramifications of not completing it. And because you know these things, you will ensure it reaches its conclusion.

If your task is part of a project, find out where it fits into the bigger picture. Don't hand it off to someone else if they offer. Unless you know you are completely out of your depth and are not capable of doing what you've been asked, never ask someone else to do it for you.

There is no upside to not owning a task. Once you become known for getting the job done, you will be top of mind when an interesting task comes along. Always jump at the opportunity.

MAKE THINGS HAPPEN
(How to avoid procrastination)

"Some people want it to happen, some wish it would happen, others make it happen."

Michael Jordan

In this age of technology, many managers do a lot of their own work but if they've hired you, they've done so in the belief that you will make their lives easier. It's not always about presentations or spreadsheets, the day to day minutiae is what they can't cope with - enter you, the trusty assistant.

As an administrator, you will be asked to make things happen. Not only that, you will be <u>expected</u> to make things happen. You are the conduit between your boss and his successful day, so learn to anticipate and facilitate.

People will turn to you when they're under pressure. Your job is to take as much pressure as possible away from them. It shouldn't be their problem if the phone system is down - until they have to approve an invoice. Work behind the scenes to get things done. You can bask in the glory later on when it's all up and running but until then, it's head down, and working like a magician (or Jesus) to perform miracles.

Some people are born with the gift of knowing how to instinctively make things happen, but I had to learn how to do it. This learning was usually as a result of a mistake. For example, the flight my boss was supposed to take was cancelled and instead of booking him on the next one immediately, I waited for his permission and he turned up a day late to his very important conference - where he was speaking.

Oh how I squirmed over that but I've never made the mistake again. If in doubt, book a flexible flight. If he's going to chew you out over the cost, it's better if he does it from the comfort of the hotel room at his destination than an uncomfortable chair in the departure lounge.

If you don't have a sense of urgency, develop it. If you're asked to fetch something don't meander slowly across the office, or stop to talk to your colleagues along the way. Walk smartly and with a purpose and concentrate on the task at hand until it's completed.

Procrastination is a writer's worst enemy so I'm very familiar with it. The funny thing is that when it comes to my day job, I never put things off. Actually, the more difficult they are, the quicker I will be to deal with them. *And get them out of the way.*

That's why I do those painful, irritating jobs first. I would rather suffer in the short term than have it hanging over me until I get around to it.

Filing is my most hated piece of office work. Thankfully, most of my filing these days is electronic but that's not the case for everyone, so don't let it pile up. It's so much worse when you have a full tray of documents that have been building up for a month, instead of just a day's worth. Yes, that's the ideal. Do it every day.

Procrastination is your enemy. A host of physical issues can be traced to that job you keep putting off. Insomnia, because you're worrying about it. Stress and anxiety because the time to get it done is running out.

If you have existing medical problems, they will be exacerbated by worries. Your relationships can be marred, both at home because you're irritable and worried, and at work, because once you've been asked a second time for that piece of work, your credibility is damaged.

Have you heard the one about the five frogs sitting on a log? One decides to jump off. How many are left? The answer is still five. Deciding to do something is not the same as actually doing it. Don't decide you're going to do that job tomorrow. Do it today.

BE INTERESTED

"The people who get on in this world are the people who get up and look for the circumstances they want, and, if they can't find them, make them."

George Bernard Shaw

A Harris Poll in 2014 identified that 36% of Americans wanted to leave their boring jobs for more creative roles. I'd go so far as to suggest that figure could be much higher. It's become quite common for women in particular to want to quit the rat race. However, this is easier said than done in most cases. Particularly since the job situation still hasn't recovered from the GFC in many places.

Did you ever wonder how a person could get excited about working in a company that makes, say, concrete tanks? I love real estate with its pretty pictures and interesting people but over the years I've worked in all sorts of industries that weren't so interesting or pretty.

I temped for a big bank in London once and it was an effort to keep my eyes open past mid-morning! For permanent roles I apply the same principles to all. Get interested. Learn about what you are working with, even if it is concrete tanks.

Learn about your customers and what they might use the tanks for. What are the consequences of their not having these tanks delivered on time? Link your products to the news - what's the talk out there in media land about concrete tanks? A Google search reveals more than fifty million results on those two words alone. There has to be something in there that will put a new spin on your industry.

You can make your day less boring by varying your tasks, offering to help out in another department and work from home on occasion if possible. Get out for a walk at lunchtime and if it's raining use the stairs, if you have one. I believe it's crucial to have an outside interest to stimulate you and that's even more important if you spend most of your day working at a boring job.

The more information you have, the less boring the job will be. Therefore, it's key to learn as much as possible about the company, its story and its products. Also, I'm very conscious that you might think concrete tanks are fascinating. The reasons for boredom are subjective and differ for everyone.

Try not to complain; it creates a negative feeling that breeds negativity around you. Develop good relationships with your co-workers - any job can be fun if you've got positive, friendly people around you. Force yourself if necessary not to clock-watch - a long day can be interminable if you're constantly checking the time. Get up, find some physical activity to do - what about that archiving you've been putting off? Before you know it, the day will have flown by.

Create challenges for yourself. It's most unlikely that an employer will complain if you find some extra work that will give you fulfilment and solve a problem for them.

If you still can't find any joy in your job you will have to dust off that Resume. Life's far too short to spend the majority of it being unhappy.

The more you invest in your work and colleagues the more benefit you will receive.

SAY YES

"If someone offers you an amazing opportunity but you are not sure you can do it, say yes - then learn how to do it later!"

Richard Branson

The quote above is one of my favourites and one I was living by even before I'd heard it.

I needed a change from secretarial work about 20 years ago and I happened to see an advert for a cook in an Irish bar in The Hague (Den Haag). I was just an okay cook but my friend gave me a reference because I'd *catered* a function for her (I got the food ready for the attendees at her father-in-law's funeral!) and a week after applying for the job, I was cooking approximately seventy Irish breakfasts a day in The Netherlands.

I had worked in hotels as a teenager and I'm a natural planner so even though I was terrified I wouldn't be able to do it; I did all right. I got fed up of the long hours and very hard work within a year but it opened other doors and I ended up back in administration, beta testing Windows 95 at Symantec.

It was a very exciting time for anyone interested in computers and it turned out to be the start of a love affair with technology that continues to this day. It was also the start of another love affair because Den Haag was where I met my husband.

All because I saw an advert in a window and thought "I could do that."

Saying yes can advance your career. I've heard it said that the Go-To person can end up saddled with 'busy work' - the stuff that other people don't want to do. I've found that work to be a welcome break at times. If it's a monotonous task it can free up your mind for other things.

If it's interesting you're getting the chance to work on something new and maybe with someone new. Straight away, you're learning new skills and growing your network. Sometimes when your first instinct is to say no, that's the very time you should say yes.

Don't put time and energy into learning how to say NO. Why would you want that negativity in your life? Learn how to say YES, it is much more exciting and fulfilling.

EMOTIONAL INTELLIGENCE

"If you are tuned out of your own emotions, you will be poor at reading them in other people."

Daniel Goleman

If your aim is to be a top PA/EA, you must develop an ability to read minds. This is called Emotional Intelligence and is not a magic trick. According to Daniel Goleman (see the Resources section at the end of this book), there are five common elements of EI.

They are self-awareness, social skills, empathy, self-regulation and self-motivation. It's easy to see that the onus is on you. If you don't have these skills, learn how to develop them. I believe the first one is most important. Know yourself. Know your strengths and weaknesses - you won't be able to read your boss if you can't read yourself.

You need these skills to read your manager and other people for whom you do work. Emotional Intelligence is about taking note of body language as well as listening to what's being said. As time goes by you learn that timing is crucial. You recognise by their body language when your boss is under pressure and you'll keep those not-so-important questions until later.

You will probably have access to their emails. In most cases, these will include personal emails so you'll understand when there may be external pressures as well as professional. If you read an email where he is expected to travel, then you will look for flights, accommodation etc. and present for their approval. Without their having to ask.

You'll learn their triggers, what annoys them, what causes them stress, and you'll learn how to cope with them. A good manager will not bring their personal problems to work but they're only human so if something has upset them out of the office, their demeanour will probably reflect this.

Try to make their day easier for them. Be kind. As a rule, we're caring, facilitating people and this is where we can shine.

Emotional Intelligence is what sets you apart. It's a leadership quality that will earn the promotion you're working towards. Learn how to develop it if you don't have it already.

HARD WORK

"The difference between ordinary and extraordinary is that little extra."

Jimmy Johnson

If you want to be successful in anything you do, you have to work hard.

I know this is also one of those subjective things but if you've got a list of tasks which are overdue, loads of emails that haven't been answered and other deadlines which haven't been met, chances are you're not working hard (or smart) enough.

Don't spend hours trying to perfect something e.g. making a presentation pretty. The content is the most important thing so get that done and hand it over to your boss and when you get some spare time you can go back to prettifying.

This is probably one of the most common traps we fall into. Spending too much time on the look of things instead of getting the content correct. If it's a complicated document, the chances are high that you will be required to make changes anyway, leave it until then to spruce it up.

Your aim is to make hard work look easy. When you're on top of your game that's how it feels and because it feels like that you tend to get even more done. Hard work not only gets you the results you need; it also gets you attention which in turn leads to chances to expand your horizons.

Don't expect the work to be easier - look to yourself to be better.

SPECIALISING

"I cannot do everything, but I can do something. I must not fail to do the something that I can do."

Helen Keller

Transitioning from a general to a specialised industry can be traumatic, soul-destroying, exhilarating and ultimately the best thing you can do for your career.

I went from being a very good all-rounder to a career in real estate where I was horrified to discover that I knew, well, basically nothing. I could type though but it's not an exaggeration to say that not every administrator could, so I wasn't completely at the bottom of the heap.

There were numerous computer programs I had never used before, but being a bit of a geek that didn't pose much of a problem. The problem was the amount of work that I didn't have time to learn before it needed to go public and that's what caused the trauma and self-doubt.

I could honestly have walked out 10 times in the first six weeks but I didn't. I got in every morning at 7am and I learned and learned until I became somewhat of an expert. I got promoted and spent a very interesting and fun six years in the business.

Don't underestimate how good you feel when you know your topic inside out. Don't underestimate how good you feel when people come to you for answers. Whether it's real estate, medical, legal or any other specialisation, there are pros and cons. Your level of expertise in the topic is high and being an expert *should* mean you get better paid than a generalist and if you're very good, you will be sought after.

On the other hand, a generalist can transfer their skills to almost all industries in many countries. You have to decide if you want to be a highly respected generalist or someone who is approached for their expertise in a certain area.

If you get the chance to move out of your department into another - say from Finance to Marketing - you should take it. Different roles in the same company are a great way to help you find your niche and also prepares you for dealing with change. Do keep in mind that it will be a big change and make sure you're prepared for it.

It is possible to transition to a specialised role with training and further learning.

FURTHER LEARNING

"Without continual growth and progress, such words as improvement, achievement, and success have no meaning."

Benjamin Franklin

Never stop learning. If your company is serious about personal development for its staff, you will have opportunities to join courses and workshops. If they don't you have to do this for yourself. Your personal development is in your own hands. Don't blame the company or your busy lifestyle for not furthering your education.

In the Resources section at the back of this book, you will find a number of companies who provide online training in almost any subject you can think of. Most are not expensive, a large number are free and there are regular sale-days where you can snap up a course on, say, Photoshop for US$10. You can't get much better than that.

"I don't need to learn Photoshop" you say. And I say to you "not today you don't, but what about that dream job you see advertised next week/month/year where Photoshop is required. Don't learn just for today. Learn for all the opportunities that are going to come your way tomorrow.

It often happens that you discover your true calling (those skills you dismissed as a hobby) when you're older and this is where you can really embrace online learning. When you learn something new, especially something that's not connected to your day job, it can be inspirational and life-changing.

Further education is not only good for your brain but it's also good for your career. It won't go unnoticed that you are eager to learn and it's always much easier to get support for your ideas and suggestions when you're willing to invest your own time to benefit the company.

If you thought you were done with learning when you left school, you can use the term **lifelong learning**. This description takes it out of the classroom and brings it into your day to day life. Is it more palatable to you now? I'm sure it sounds better.

Lifelong learning opens your mind and the more you learn, the more you will want to learn, I can testify to this too. People who participate in online courses can, and do, study more than one subject at a time.

Don't stop your learning when children come along - sometimes that might keep you sane! If you have to take a break, make sure you come back to it.

You will never be kinder to your brain than when you're learning something new.

STRESS

"Stress is nothing more than a socially acceptable form of mental illness."

Richard Carlson

I love that quote, all the more because it's true. We wear stress like badges of honour. As if to have a relaxing environment is to make us of less value somehow.

Not true. A happy, relaxed, stress-free individual on top of their game will be of more value to themselves and their company than any burned-out husk of a person.

That's not to say that <u>some</u> stress is actually good for you. It gets your adrenalin flowing and at times you will find yourself coming up with ideas that you wouldn't have otherwise.

Many of us cause our own stress. We put unrealistic expectations on ourselves. I don't believe in 'learning how to say no'. We're employed to do a job and we have to do it. What we can do is learn how to prioritise and work to that.

Anyone with unrealistic expectations (i.e. if it doesn't have a deadline and the other work you're doing has) should be told, politely and firmly, that you are busy right now but you will get to it as soon as possible.

Actually, start with 'I'll do it as soon as I can, but........". This is really important - you must try to always start your statements/sentences with a positive. That way they're focusing on how you're going to help them and not on the negative part of your sentence. In my experience this will give you space to get your work done.

Ask yourself if you are feeling stress because of what you are actually doing or is there a possibility that you're stressed because you anticipated you would be? And is it always bad for you? Stress triggers our <u>fight or flight</u> sensors which can in turn trigger our creativity, our capability, our confidence even. Just as it is with most things in life, you don't need nor want too much of it but in moderation it can be positive.

If you don't fear being stressed, chances are you will be able to deal with stressful situations more easily.

You don't <u>have</u> to be stressed to be good at your job. If you're not stressed that doesn't mean you're not busy.

Remember, our attitude at the start of a task can determine the outcome, therefore promise yourself you will get the job done without stress. You might surprise yourself.

BEST FOOT FORWARD

"I know you've heard it a thousand times before. But it's true - hard work pays off. If you want to be good you have to practice, practice, practice. If you don't love something, then don't do it."

Ray Bradbury

I hope this book has given you the tools, and ideas to go with them, that will help you be a Go-To person. If you work for a large organisation you won't be the only one, so get some tips from them if you can. Ask if you can shadow them for a day as they go about their work.

Being a secretary/assistant/administrator can be a thankless task at times, depending on who you work for. Your main trumpet-blower will be yourself.

Do not become a martyr and let others take credit for the work you do. If you're going to own an outcome that's less than favourable, make sure you own the successes as well.

Being kind is key to your success in a secretarial role. Being able to listen and learn is of equal importance. I don't believe you can be a respected, successful secretary if you don't have both.

Even if you dislike your boss your next promotion depends on him or her - be nice to them. You have to get on with him and work to his schedule, not the other way round.

Don't speak badly about them. Do your job to the very, very best of your ability especially if you know you're not going to stay.

It's always better to be missed than dismissed.

Administrators are hired because they know how to do something better than their boss does. Don't disrespect them for this. It's a sign of good management.

Be the best you can be, for yourself first and then everyone else. If you follow the suggestions here, you will have a more fulfilling job which will lead to a more fulfilling life.

RESOURCES

Mindtools - www.mindtools.com

Learn hundreds of useful career skills

Lifehack - www.lifehack.org

Techniques to help manage your time and your technology

Udemy - www.udemy.com

Online learning where experts from many disciplines can create courses

Coursera - www.coursera.com

Online learning site offering Massive Open Online Courses (MOOC)

Forbes - www.forbes.com

Business and technology information from Forbes Magazine

TED Talk: How to make stress your friend

http://bit.ly/1MNCUaZ

Harvard study 2013 about the power of Because

https://bitly.com/

Shorten long website links

Daniel Goleman – Emotional Intelligence

http://www.danielgoleman.info/topics/emotional-intelligence/

www.ingramcontent.com/pod-product-compliance
Lightning Source LLC
Chambersburg PA
CBHW021014180526
45163CB00005B/1953